Design: Art of Design
Recipe Photography: Peter Barry
Jacket and Illustration Artwork: Jane Winton, courtesy
of Bernard Thornton Artists, London
Editors: Jillian Stewart and Kate Cranshaw

CLB 3522
Published by Grange Books, an imprint of Grange Books
PLC, The Grange, Grange Yard, London, SE1 3AG
© 1994 CLB Publishing, Godalming, Surrey, England.
All rights reserved
Printed and bound in Singapore
Published 1994
ISBN 1-85627-454-3

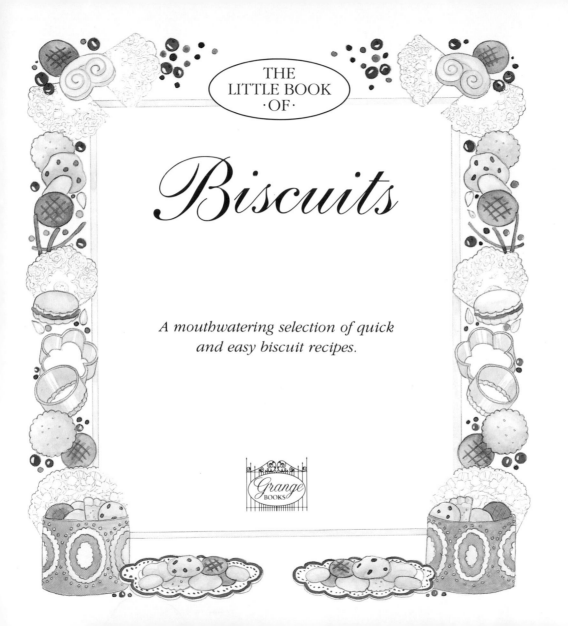

THE LITTLE BOOK ·OF·

Biscuits

*A mouthwatering selection of quick
and easy biscuit recipes.*

Grange
BOOKS

Introduction

Tasty though they may be, bought biscuits are no match for the homemade variety. Fresh from the oven, home-baked biscuits crumble in the mouth, and have the good, wholesome flavour that all those chemical additives seem to obliterate in commercially made foods. Excellent, too, are home-baked savoury crackers, which are particularly impressive at dinner parties.

Biscuits are fun to experiment with and quite adaptable when it comes to making your own changes. Your own biscuits do not have to be as sweet as bought ones, which are usually packed with sugar. Of particular interest to those following a low-cholesterol diet or one free of dairy products is the fact that you can choose the type of fat used, and although butter is generally believed to give the best taste, margarines are an excellent substitute.

Most people are surprised at how easy and quick biscuits are to make. It is just a matter of mixing the ingredients together, rolling out the dough and cutting the shapes, or simply putting spoonfuls of mixture onto a baking tray. And baking often takes

less than 15 minutes. On those days when there are no biscuits in the cupboard, it can actually be quicker to make a quick batch than to go out and buy a packet. The smell of baking is wonderful, too, and in a houseful of children this will soon bring expectant faces around the kitchen table.

The rolling out and cutting of biscuit shapes is a simple and satisfying activity, and one in which children love to help. Stars, crescents and novelty shapes all lend themselves to biscuits, and somehow they look so much more appetising to children than do the simple flat circles.

Biscuits are dainty and more delicate than cake, and can look particularly attractive served on an interesting dish. They can also make an imaginative gift, layered in a homemade box and tied with attractive ribbon. What better present could there be for a grandmother or aunt? Stored in an airtight container, most biscuits will keep well for weeks.

This selection of recipes offers traditional favourites as well as the more unusual varieties. Try baking your own cookies, and you'll soon discover just how delicious the results can be.

Walnut Sultana Biscuits

MAKES 36 BISCUITS

Use your favourite dried fruit and nuts to vary these delicious biscuits.

PREPARATION: 15 mins
COOKING: 8-10 mins

225g/8oz butter
340g/12oz demarara sugar
3 eggs
1 tsp bicarbonate soda dissolved in 1½ tbsps
   hot water
370g/13oz plain flour, sieved
½ tsp salt
1 tsp cinnamon
120g/4oz walnuts, chopped
150g/5oz sultanas

---

1. Cream the butter and sugar together in a mixing bowl until light and fluffy.

2. Beat in the eggs one at a time, beating well in between each addition.

3. Add the soda mixture, then work in half of the flour, together with the salt and cinnamon.

4. Mix in the walnuts and sultanas, then the remaining flour.

5. Grease several baking sheets and drop the mixture on by spoonfuls about 2.5cm/1-inch apart.

6. Bake in an oven preheated to 180°C/350°F/ Gas Mark 4, for about 8-10 minutes, or until golden brown.

7. Remove from the trays with a palette knife and cool on a wire rack.

Brown Sugar Biscuits

MAKES ABOUT 36

These crisp biscuits are perfect as an accompaniment to ice cream or fruit salad.

PREPARATION: 20 mins
COOKING: 10-12 mins

275g/10oz demerara sugar
3 tbsps golden syrup
60ml/4 tbsps water
1 egg
250g/9oz plain flour
1 tbsp ground ginger
1 tbsp bicarbonate of soda
Pinch salt
120g/4oz finely chopped nuts

---

1. Mix the sugar, syrup, water and egg together in a large bowl. Beat with an electric mixer until pale and thick.

2. Sift flour with the ginger, bicarbonate of soda and salt into the brown sugar mixture and add the nuts. Stir by hand until thoroughly mixed.

Step 1 Combine the sugar, syrup, water and egg with an electric mixer until light.

Step 3 Use a spoon to drop the batter about 5cm/2 inches apart onto a greased baking sheet.

3. Lightly oil three baking sheets and drop the mixture on by spoonfuls about 5cm/2 inches apart.

4. Bake in an oven pre-heated to 190°C/375°F/Gas Mark 5 for about 10-12 minutes, or until lightly browned around the edges. Leave on the baking sheet for 1-2 minutes before removing with a palette knife to a wire rack to cool completely.

Step 4 Bake until browned around the edges. Cool slightly and remove with a palette knife.

11

Sand Biscuits

MAKES 36

These lovely, rich biscuits get their name from the French word sable, meaning sand.

PREPARATION: 20 mins plus, chilling
COOKING: 10 mins

225g/8oz granulated sugar
225g/8oz butter
1 egg, beaten
225g/8oz plain flour
1 egg white, slightly beaten
Caster sugar
Finely chopped pecans or walnuts

1. Cream the sugar and butter together until light and fluffy. Beat in the egg and gradually add the flour, working it in well to make a stiff dough. Not all the flour may be needed.

2. Chill the mixture overnight, or until firm enough to roll out. Roll the dough out in small portions on a well floured surface. Cut into 5-7.5cm/2-3 inch circles with a biscuit cutter.

3. Place on greased baking sheets. Brush the tops with the beaten egg white and sprinkle with a mixture of sugar and finely chopped nuts.

4. Bake in an oven preheated to 180°C/350°F/Gas Mark 4, for about 10 minutes, or until crisp and pale golden. Leave a few minutes on the baking sheets then remove to wire cooling racks.

Pecan Pastries

MAKES 12

These sweet, nutty pastries are deep-fried to make them light and crisp.

PREPARATION: 30 mins
COOKING: 25 mins

120g/4oz plain flour
1 tsp baking powder
¼ tsp salt
60ml/4 tbsps cold water
Oil for deep frying
280ml/½ pint golden syrup mixed with 140ml/
    ¼ pint treacle
90g/3oz finely chopped pecans

---

1. Sift the flour, baking powder and salt together into a large bowl. Make a well in the centre and pour in the cold water.

2. Using a wooden spoon, mix until a stiff dough forms, and then knead by hand until smooth.

Step 1 Sift the dry ingredients into a bowl and make a well in the centre.

Step 3 On a floured surface, roll out each piece until very thin.

3. Divide the dough into 12 portions, each about the size of a walnut. Roll out each portion of dough on a floured surface until very thin.

4. Heat the oil in a deep-fat fryer to 180°C/350°F. Drop each piece of pastry into the hot fat using two forks. Twist the pastry just as it hits the oil. Cook one at a time until light brown.

5. In a large saucepan, boil the syrup until it reaches 239°F/115°C on a sugar thermometer, or forms a soft ball when dropped into cold water.

6. Drain the pastries on kitchen paper after frying and dip carefully into the hot syrup. Sprinkle with pecans before the syrup sets and allow to cool before serving.

Coconut Tile Biscuits

MAKES 30

These home-made biscuits provide the perfect finishing touch to a wide variety of desserts, especially ice creams or sorbets.

PREPARATION: 10 mins
COOKING: 35 mins

120g/4oz sugar
2 egg whites
60g/2oz plain flour
60g/2oz butter, melted
45g/1½oz desiccated coconut, ground

---

1. Beat the sugar into the egg whites. Add the flour and butter, beating well. Beat in the coconut, then allow to rest for 10 minutes.

2. Butter some baking sheets and use the back of a spoon to spread out 1 tbsp of batter for each biscuit.

3. Cook each tray for 3-4 minutes in an oven

Step 3 Remove the biscuits from the tray with a palette knife.

preheated to 200°C/400°F/Gas Mark 6. Remove the biscuits from the trays with a palette knife and immediately shape them around a rolling pin. They will cool and harden very quickly. Slide onto a wire rack to cool.

4. Repeat the cooking and cooling operation until all the batter has been used up.

Step 2 Spread out about 1 tbsp of batter for each biscuit.

Step 3 Immediately shape the cooked biscuits around a rolling pin.

Shortbread Biscuits

MAKES ABOUT 18

Sandwich these biscuits together with raspberry jam for children's parties.

PREPARATION: 10 mins
COOKING: 10-15 mins

150g/5oz white flour
75g/2½oz light muscovado sugar, finely ground
120g/4oz soft margarine
½ tsp vanilla essence

---

1. Sieve the flour and sugar together and rub in the margarine.

2. Add the vanilla essence and bind the mixture together.

3. Form into small balls and place on a baking tray a few inches apart.

4. With the back of a fork, press the balls down making a criss-cross pattern.

5. Bake in an oven preheated to 190°C/375°F/Gas Mark 4, for about 10-15 minutes until golden brown in colour.

6. Cool and store in an airtight container.

Macaroons

MAKES ABOUT 24

Serve these delicious chewy almond biscuits with tea or coffee.

PREPARATION: 15 mins, plus 15 mins standing
COOKING: 15-20 mins

225g/8oz whole almonds
225g/8oz granulated sugar
2 egg whites
1 tsp almond essence

1. Blanch the almonds by plunging them into boiling water for 2 minutes.

2. Skin the almonds and spread them over a baking sheet.

3. Dry off in a warm oven for a few minutes without browning.

4. Grind the granulated sugar until it resembles fine caster sugar.

5. Grind the almonds.

6. Sieve the sugar and almonds together.

7. In a large bowl, beat the egg whites until stiff but not dry.

8. Gradually fold in the almond and sugar mixture using a metal tablespoon and add the almond essence.

9. Pipe or spoon the mixture onto a floured baking sheet, alternatively put the mixture on to sheets of edible rice paper.

10. Leave for 10-15 minutes to rest before baking.

11. Bake in an oven preheated to 180°C/350°F/Gas Mark 4, for 15-20 minutes until golden brown.

12. Transfer the cooked macaroons to a cooling rack.

Peanut Butter Bran Cookies

MAKES ABOUT 35

These rich, crumbly cookies are just the thing for hungry children, and make a good mid-morning snack with a glass of milk.

PREPARATION: 15 mins
COOKING: 10 mins

120g/4oz butter or margarine
120g/4oz light muscovado sugar
1 egg, beaten
225g/8oz crunchy peanut butter
60g/2oz bran
120g/4oz wholemeal flour
Pinch salt
½ tsp baking powder
½ tsp vanilla essence

---

1. Beat together the butter and sugar until pale

Step 2 Beat the peanut butter into the creamed mixture.

Step 2 Add the bran, flour, salt, soda and essence to the peanut mixture, stirring well to make a stiff dough.

and creamy. Gradually add the egg, beating well after each addition.

2. Beat in the peanut butter, bran, flour, salt, baking powder and essence, mixing well to form a stiff dough.

3. Take small pieces of the dough and roll into balls. Place well apart on two greased baking sheets and flatten slightly with a fork or palette knife.

4. Bake one tray at time, in an oven preheated to 190°C/375°F/Gas Mark 5, for 5-10 minutes. Cool slightly on the tray then transfer to a wire rack to cool completely.

Sunflower Chocolate Cookies

MAKES ABOUT 28

The addition of sunflower seeds to these cookies adds texture as well as a lovely flavour.

PREPARATION: 20 mins
COOKING: 10 mins

120g/4oz butter or margarine
120g/4oz light muscovado sugar
1 egg, beaten
1 tsp vanilla essence
½ tsp bicarbonate of soda
½ tsp salt
30g/1oz bran
90g/3oz rolled oats
120g/4oz wholemeal flour
60g/2oz sunflower seeds
120g/4oz chocolate chips

1. Beat together the butter and sugar until pale and creamy. Gradually add the egg, beating well after each addition.

2. Beat in the vanilla essence, then beat in the bicarbonate of soda, salt, bran, oats and flour, mixing well until a stiff dough is produced.

3. Finally beat in the sunflower seeds and chocolate chips.

4. Place heaped spoonfuls of the mixture onto two greased baking sheets and bake in an oven preheated to 190°C/375°F/Gas Mark 5, for 5-10 minutes.

5. Cool slightly on the tray then transfer to a wire rack to cool completely.

Muesli Cookies

MAKES ABOUT 36

These simple-to-make biscuits are full of wholesome ingredients.

PREPARATION: 15 mins
COOKING: 20 mins

120g/4oz butter or margarine
120g/4oz light muscovado sugar
1 egg, beaten
1 tsp vanilla essence
1 tsp baking powder
225g/8oz wholemeal flour
Pinch salt
120g/4oz muesli
60g/2oz currants

Step 2 Mix the dry ingredients and fruit into the egg mixture to form a stiff dough.

1. Beat together the butter and sugar until pale and creamy. Gradually add the egg, beating well after each addition.

2. Beat in the vanilla essence, then beat in the baking powder, flour, salt, muesli and currants to make a stiff dough.

3. Place heaped spoonfuls of the mixture on to two greased baking sheets and bake in an oven preheated to 190°C/375°F/Gas Mark 5, for 5-10 minutes.

4. Cool slightly on the tray then transfer to a wire rack to cool completely.

Lemon-Iced Treacle Cookies

MAKES ABOUT 30

Children in particular will love these little biscuits.

PREPARATION: 20 mins
COOKING: 30 mins

120g/4oz butter or margarine
120g/4oz light muscovado sugar
1 egg, beaten
2 tbsps treacle
2 tsps baking powder
1 tsp ground allspice
½ tsp ground ginger
225g/8oz wholemeal flour
Pinch salt
460g/1lb icing sugar
Grated rind and juice 1 lemon
Yellow food colouring (optional)
Candied lemon slices (optional)
140ml/¼ pint water

---

1. Beat together the butter and sugar until pale and creamy. Gradually add the egg, beating well after each addition.

2. Beat in the treacle, then using a metal spoon fold in the baking powder, spices, flour and salt.

Step 1 Cream the sugar and butter together in a large bowl until they become fluffy and light in texture.

3. Place spoonfuls of the mixture onto two greased baking sheets and bake one tray at a time for 5-10 minutes in an oven preheated to 190°C/375°F/Gas Mark 5.

4. Cool slightly on the tray then transfer to a wire rack to cool completely.

5. When all the biscuits are cooked, sieve the icing sugar into a bowl and add the lemon rind and juice. Add colouring if using.

6. Gradually stir in enough water to form a thin coating icing and spread equal amounts onto each biscuit. Decorate if wished and allow the icing to set before serving.

Langues de Chat

SERVES 6

'Cat's tongues' are a classic accompaniment to ice cream or fruit desserts, and are also traditionally served with afternoon tea.

PREPARATION: 15 mins
COOKING: 10-15 mins

165g/5½oz softened butter
250g/9oz icing sugar
1 tsp vanilla essence
5 egg whites
225g/8oz plain flour, sifted

---

1. Cream the butter with the icing sugar and the vanilla essence. Add the egg whites one by one, alternating with the flour until a firm dough is obtained.

2. Place the dough in an icing bag fitted with a plain nozzle. Pipe even-sized strips of dough onto a greased baking sheet. Leave space between the biscuits as they spread during baking.

Step 2 Pipe even-sized strips of dough onto a greased baking sheet, leaving plenty of space between each.

3. Bake in an oven preheated to 200°C/400°F/ Gas Mark 6 for 10-15 minutes: the edges should be golden brown but the centres still light.

4. When cooked, remove the biscuits from the oven, allow them to cool slightly on the baking sheet, then use a palette knife to lift them onto a wire rack. Allow them to cool completely.

Step 2 Spoon the biscuit dough into an icing bag fitted with a plain nozzle.

Step 4 When cooked and slightly cooled, remove the biscuits to a cooling rack using a palette knife.

Oatlet Cookies

MAKES 10

A delicious mix of oats, seeds and syrup makes these cookies extra special.

PREPARATION: 15 mins
COOKING: 10 mins

120g/4oz porridge oats
120g/4oz plain flour
90g/3oz sunflower seeds
30g/1oz sesame seeds
½ tsp mixed spice
120g/4oz butter or margarine
1 tbsp brown sugar
1 tsp golden syrup or molasses
½ tsp baking powder
1 tbsp boiling water
225g/8oz chocolate chips

1. Mix the oats, flour, sunflower seeds, sesame seeds and spice together.

2. Melt the butter, sugar and golden syrup or molasses over a gentle heat.

3. Add the baking powder and water to the syrup mixture and stir well.

4. Pour over the dry ingredients and mix well.

5. Place spoonfuls of the mixture well apart onto a greased baking tray and bake in an oven preheated to 190°C/375°F/Gas Mark 5, for 10 minutes.

6. Allow to cool on the tray.

7. Melt the chocolate chips in a bowl over hot water and place teaspoonsful on top of the cookies. Leave to set. Store in an airtight tin.

33

Ginger Nuts

MAKES 36

These spicy biscuits are given a delicious texture by including nuts in the recipe.

PREPARATION: 20 mins
COOKING: 10 mins

175g/6oz butter or margarine
120g/4oz dark muscovado sugar
120ml/4 fl oz treacle
2 tsps vinegar
3 eggs, beaten
2 tbsps milk
680g/1½lbs wholemeal flour
1½ tsps bicarbonate soda
2 tsp ground ginger
½ tsp ground cinnamon
Pinch ground cloves
60g/2oz hazelnuts, chopped

Step 2 Make a firm dough by beating the dry ingredients into the treacle mixture and mixing well with a wooden spoon.

1. Put the butter, sugar, treacle and vinegar into a large mixing bowl and beat together well until they are smooth and well blended.

2. Beat in the eggs and milk. Add the flour, bicarbonate of soda, spices and hazelnuts, mixing well to form a firm dough.

3. Take small amounts of the biscuit mixture and roll into balls. Place well apart on two greased baking sheets.

4. Press each biscuit down with a fork and bake in an oven preheated to 190°C/375°F/Gas Mark 5, for 5-10 minutes.

5. Cool slightly on the tray then transfer to a wire rack to cool completely.

Step 1 Beat the butter, sugar, treacle and vinegar together in a large bowl until they are smooth and well blended.

Old-Style Molasses Cookies

MAKES ABOUT 45

To make the preparation of these cookies easier, weigh the molasses directly into the saucepan.

PREPARATION: 10 mins
COOKING: 8-12 mins

150g/5oz sugar
175g/6oz molasses
150g/5oz butter
150ml/5 fl oz buttermilk
340g/12oz flour
1 tsp bicarbonate of soda
2 tsps cinnamon
1 tsp ginger
½ tsp cloves
½ tsp nutmeg
½ tsp salt
175g/6oz raisins, chopped

1. Place the sugar, molasses and butter in a large, heavy-based pan and cook, stirring, until the mixture comes to the boil.

2. Allow to boil for 1 minute, then remove from the heat and stir in the buttermilk.

3. Sift together the flour, bicarbonate of soda, spices and salt, and beat this thoroughly into the molasses mixture. Stir in the raisins.

4. Drop teaspoonfuls of the mixture onto greased baking sheets, leaving plenty of space between them, and bake in an oven preheated to 180°C/350°F/Gas Mark 4 for 8-12 minutes.

5. When cooked, allow to cool slightly, before removing to a cake tray to cool completely.

Palmiers

These delicious biscuits originated in France, where they are sold in pâtisseries all over the country.

PREPARATION: 15 mins, plus chilling
COOKING: 20 mins

225g/8oz puff pastry
3 tbsps caster sugar
Icing sugar

1. Roll the puff pastry out to form a rectangle 30.5cm/12 inches long and 3mm/⅛-inch thick.

2. Sprinkle a work surface with half the caster sugar. Place the dough on the sugared surface, and sprinkle over the remaining sugar. Roll lightly over the dough so that the sugar sticks to it.

3. Roll each of the two short ends of the dough up toward the middle, and place the rolled dough in the freezer for 20 minutes, to make it easier to slice.

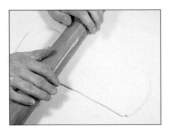

Step 1 Roll the dough out to a rectangle, about 30.5cm/12 inches long and 3mm/ ⅛ inch thick.

Step 3 Roll up the ends of the dough towards the middle.

4. Remove from the freezer and slice the rolled dough to the preferred thickness.

5. Place the biscuits on a dampened baking sheet. Bake in an oven preheated to 200°C/400°F/Gas Mark 6, for 20 minutes, or until golden brown.

6. Allow the palmiers to cool, then sprinkle with icing sugar before serving.

Step 4 Cut the chilled dough into slices.

Susan's Oaties

MAKES ABOUT 20

For a super taste add finely chopped nuts or desiccated coconut to this recipe.

PREPARATION: 10 mins
COOKING: 20 mins

120g/4oz butter or margarine
120g/4oz brown sugar
1 tsp molasses
1 tsp boiling water
1 tsp bicarbonate of soda
120g/4oz wholemeal flour
120g/4oz oats
½ tsp baking powder

---

1. Melt the butter, sugar and molasses in a saucepan.

2. Add the boiling water and bicarbonate of soda.

3. Remove from the heat and stir in the flour, oats and baking powder.

4. Place teaspoons of the mixture onto greased baking sheets.

5. Bake in an oven preheated to 160°C/325°F/ Gas Mark 3, for 20 minutes.

6. Remove from the baking sheets and place on a wire tray to cool.

Hermits

MAKES ABOUT 50

Replace the allspice and raisins with cinnamon and chopped nuts for another tasty version.

PREPARATION: 15-20 mins
COOKING: 12-15 mins

120g/4oz butter
225g/8oz sugar
120ml/4 fl oz milk
225g/8oz plain flour
1 tsp allspice
½ tsp bicarbonate of soda
½ tsp cream of tartar
90g/3oz raisins

1. Cream the butter and sugar together until pale and fluffy, then gradually beat in the milk.

2. Sift together the flour, allspice, bicarbonate of soda and cream of tartar.

3. Add the flour mixture to the butter mixture, beating well after each addition until the batter is smooth.

4. Chop the raisins and stir them into the batter.

5. Drop teaspoonsful of the batter onto greased baking sheets, spacing them well apart.

6. Bake in an oven preheated to 190°C/375°F/Gas Mark 5, for 12-15 minutes.

7. Allow to cool slightly before removing to a wire tray to cool completely.

Index

Brown Sugar Biscuits 10
Coconut Tile Biscuits 16
Ginger Nuts 34
Hermits 42
Langues de Chat 30
Lemon Iced Treacle Cookies 28
Macaroons 20
Muesli Cookies 26
Oatlet Cookies 32

Old-Style Molasses Cookies 36
Palmiers 38
Peanut Butter Bran Cookies 22
Pecan Pastries 14
Sand Biscuits 12
Shortbread Biscuits 18
Sunflower Chocolate Cookies 24
Susan's Oaties 40
Walnut Sultana Biscuits 8